CONTRIBUTIONS BY
Rachel Jankovic, Gloria Furman
Rachel Pieh Jones, Christine Hoover,
Carolyn McCulley, Trillia Newbell
AND Christina Fox

ılıı

MOM

THE FEARLESS MOTHER'S HEART AND HOPE

ENOUGH

EDITED BY

Tony and Karalee Reinke

ılıı

© 2014 Desiring God

Published by Desiring God
Post Office Box 2901
Minneapolis, MN 55402

www.desiringGod.org

COVER DESIGN AND TYPESETTING
Peter Voth

Table of Contents

Contributors

CHRISTINA FOX (@ToShowThemJesus) is a homeschooling mom, licensed mental health counselor, and writer. She lives in south Florida with her husband of seventeen years and their two boys. She shares her faith journey at toshowthemJesus.com.

GLORIA FURMAN (@GloriaFurman) lives in Dubai with her husband Dave, a pastor, and their four young kids. Gloria is the author of three books: *Glimpses of Grace: Treasuring the Gospel in Your Home* (2013), *Treasuring Christ When Your Hands Are Full: Gospel Meditations for Busy Moms* (2014), and *The Pastor's Wife* (2015). For more see gloriafurman.com.

CHRISTINE HOOVER (@ChristineHoover) is the wife of a church planting pastor and stay-at-home mom to their three boys. She is the author of three books: *The Church Planting Wife: Help and Hope for Her Heart* (2013), *Partners in Ministry: Help and Encouragement for Ministry Wives* (2014), and *From Good to Grace: Letting Go of the Goodness Gospel* (2015). She enjoys helping other ministry wives embrace God's calling on their lives through her blog, gracecoversme.com.

RACHEL JANKOVIC (@LizzieJank) is a wife, homemaker, and mother of six. She's the author of two books: *Loving the Little Years: Motherhood in the Trenches* (2010) and *Fit to Burst: Abundance, Mayhem, and the Joys of Motherhood* (2013). She blogs at feminagirls.com.

RACHEL PIEH JONES (@RachelPiehJones) is a wife, mother of three, and freelance writer. She lives in East Africa and blogs at djiboutijones.com.

CAROLYN MCCULLEY (@CarolynMcCulley) is the founder of Citygate Films and the director/producer of the Desiring God short film, The Story of Ian and Larissa. She is the author of three books, including: *Radical Womanhood: Feminine Faith in a Feminist World* (2008) and *The Measure of Success: Uncovering the Biblical Perspective on Women, Work, and the Home* (2014). For more see carolynmcculley.com.

TRILLIA NEWBELL (@TrilliaNewbell) is a wife and mother of two who lives in Nashville. She's the author of two books: *United: Captured by God's Vision for Diversity* (2014) and *Fear and Faith* (2015). For more see trillianewbell.com.

Editor's Preface

"Are you mom enough?" The haunting question hung in bold red text over a startling picture of a mother breast-feeding her four-year-old son on the May 2012 cover of *Time Magazine*. The issue hit newsstands and re-ignited a longstanding mommy war in American culture. We were ready to respond from a Christian perspective at desiring-God.org—but only barely.

Ten months earlier (July 2011), when our blog was just beginning to take shape and we had no regular female contributors, writer and mother of six, Rachel Jankovic (Idaho), wrote and emailed a submission to us in a Word doc. We pasted it into a blog post, gave it a simple title—"Motherhood Is a Calling (And Where Your Children Rank)"—and hit *publish*. We simply posted the text and added no image, no color, no visual flair. Despite its minimalism, the post spread virally immediately, and the initial momentum swelled for months. A full three years later, the post has been 'liked' on Facebook over 100,000 times and viewed over 500,000 times, both records for anything published on the Desiring God blog. The post now averages 180 visits every day.

Rachel's post awoke us to the segment of DG blog readers who are wives and mothers eager to apply the gospel to their hearts and homes. Sensing the need, in February of 2012 I wrote in my journal a short prayer: "We need more 'mommy bloggers' who can write, who have time to write, and, most importantly, who understand the gospel, joy, and Christian Hedonism, and who are skilled to apply all this to their own hearts in the context of the home and the pressures of motherhood." It was a prayer echoed verbally many times by the content team here at DG. In the meantime, Rachel was kind enough to continue writing for us. As a team we began reading mommy blogs, gathering leads, and sending requests.

In March 2012, we received our first posts from Rachel Pieh Jones (Djibouti) and Christine Hoover (Virginia). The next month we added to the mix Gloria Furman (Dubai) and Trillia Newbell (Tennessee). In June we published a post from Rebekah Merkle (Idaho). In 2013 we began receiving posts from Christina Fox (Florida) and Stacy Reaoch (Pennsylvania).

Without intending it, this geographically diverse group of women created a unique, global perspective on biblical femininity. Spread across the country and across the world, these ladies shared one calling: seeking to live fruitfully and faithfully as daughters of God, wives, and moms.

The two-year span between March 2012 and March 2014 brackets a golden age of blog publishing for us. These writers combined to publish 89 posts, mostly under the banner: "Grace at Home." They addressed themes like the mother's struggle with anxiety, the crucial value of prayer, treasuring children, the challenges of perfectionism, the lies of feminism, the loss of promising careers, dependence on God, and the ugly pride behind mommy wars.

Christian mothers today find themselves pitched in a battle that will not end until Christ returns, so DG's female contributors continue to play an essential role in our online voice. But we have found a place more naturally integrated into the overall flow of our content. This spring we retired the "Grace at Home" label, and now look back on it as a banner over God's overwhelmingly gracious answer to our prayers.

Mom Enough is a compilation of the most popular pieces from this golden age, here published in chronological order. As you will see, the aim of *Mom Enough* is not to boost a mother's self-sufficiency, but to build her fearlessness as she finds her sufficiency outside of herself (1 Pet. 3:1–6). This paradox is the secret power of godly mothers. Becoming mom enough comes as a result of answering the question, "Are you mom enough?," with a firm *no*.

We begin with the blog post from Rachel Jankovic that started it all.

Tony Reinke
October 2014
desiringGod.org

01 Motherhood Is a Calling
(And Where Your Children Rank)

RACHEL JANKOVIC

A few years ago, when I had only four children and when the oldest was still three, I loaded them all up to go on a walk. After the final sippy cup found a place and we were ready to go, my two-year-old turned to me and said, "Wow! You have your hands full!"

She could have just as well said, "Don't you know what causes that?" or "Are they all yours?!"

Everywhere you go, people want to talk about your children. Why you shouldn't have had them, how you could have prevented them, and why they would never do what you have done. They want to make sure you know that you won't be smiling anymore when they are teenagers. And they say all this in line at the grocery store while your children listen.

A Rock-Bottom Job?

Years ago, before this generation of mothers was even born, our society decided where children rank in the list of important things. When abortion was legalized, we wrote it into law.

Children rank way below college. Below world travel. Below nightlife. Below physical fitness. Below a career. In fact, children rate below your desire to sit around and pick your toes, if that is what you want to do. Below everything. Children are the last thing you should ever spend your time doing.

If you grew up in this culture, it is very hard to get a biblical perspective on motherhood. How much do we listen to partial truths and half lies? Do we believe that we want children because there is some biological urge, or a phantom "baby itch"? Are we really in this because of cute clothes and photo opportunities? Is motherhood a rock-bottom job for those who can't do more, or for those who are satisfied with drudgery? If so, what are we thinking?

It's Not a Hobby

Motherhood is not a hobby, it's a calling. You do not collect children because you find them cuter than stamps. You do not raise children if you can squeeze the time in. Motherhood is what God gave you time for.

Christian mothers carry their children in hostile territory. When you are in public with them, you are standing with, and defending, the objects of cultural dislike. You are publicly testifying that you value what God values, and that you refuse to value what the world values. You stand with the defenseless and in front of the needy. You represent everything that our culture hates, because you represent laying down your life for another—and laying down your life for another represents the gospel.

Our culture is afraid of death. Laying down your own life, in any way, is terrifying. Strangely, it is that fear that drives the abortion industry: fear that your dreams will die, that your future will die, and that your freedom will die. Abortion tries to escape that death by running into the arms of death.

Run to the Cross

But Christians should have a different paradigm. We should run to the cross. To death. So lay down your hopes. Lay down your future. Lay down your petty annoyances. Lay down your desire to be recognized. Lay down your fussiness at your children. Lay down your perfectly clean house. Lay down your grievances about the life you are living. Lay down the imaginary life you could have by yourself. Lay them all down.

Death to yourself is not the end of the story. We, of all people, ought to know what follows death. The Christian life is a resurrection life, a life that cannot be contained by death, a life only possible when you have been to the cross and back.

The Bible is clear about the value of children. Jesus loves them, and we are commanded to love them, to bring them up in the nurture of the Lord. We are to imitate God and take pleasure in our children.

The Question Is How

The question here is not *if* you are representing the gospel, but *how* you are representing it. Do you give your life to your children resentfully? Do you tally everything you do for them like a loan shark tallies debts? Or do you give them life the way God gives it to us—freely?

It isn't enough to pretend, though you might fool a few people. That person in line at the store might believe you when you plaster on a fake smile, but your children won't. They know exactly where they stand with you. They know the things that you rate above them. They know everything you resent and hold against them. They know that you faked a cheerful answer to that lady, only to whisper threats or bark at them in the car.

Children know the difference between a mother who is saving her face to a stranger and a mother who is defending her children's lives with her smile, her love, and her absolute loyalty.

Hands Full of Good Things

When my little girl told me, "Your hands are full!" I was so thankful that she already knew what my answer would be. It was the same one that I always give: "Yes, they are—full of good things!"

Live the gospel in the things that no one sees. Sacrifice for your children in places that only they will know. Put their value ahead of yours. Grow them up in the clean air of gospel living. Your testimony to the gospel in the little details of your life is more valuable to them than you can imagine. If you tell them the gospel, but live to yourself, they will never believe it. Give your life for theirs every day, joyfully. Lay down pettiness. Lay down fussiness. Lay down resentment about the dishes, about the laundry, about how no one knows how hard you work.

Stop clinging to yourself and cling to the cross. There is more joy and more life and more laughter on the other side of death than you can possibly carry alone.

02 Motherhood Is a Mission Field

RACHEL JANKOVIC

There is a good old saying that distance adds intrigue. It is certainly true—just think back to anything that has ever been distant from you that is now near. Your driver's license. Marriage. Children. Things that used to seem so fascinating, but as they drew near become less mystical and more, well, *real*.

This same principle also applies to mission fields. The closer you get to home, the less intriguing the work of sacrifice seems. As another good old saying goes, "Everyone wants to save the world, but no one wants to help Mom with the dishes." When you are a mother at home with your children, the church is not clamoring for monthly ministry updates. When you talk to other believers, they don't communicate awe about what you are sacrificing for the gospel. People do not press you for needs they can fill for you, or how they can pray for you. Your life does not feel intriguing, or glamorous. Your work is normal, because you are as close to home as you can possibly be. You have actually gone so far as to *become* home.

The Headwaters of Mission

If you are a Christian woman who loves the Lord, the gospel is important to you. It is easy to become discouraged, thinking that the work you are doing does not matter much. If you were really doing something for Christ you would be out there, somewhere else, doing it. Even if you have a great perspective on your role in the kingdom, it is easy to lose sight of it in the mismatched socks, in the morning sickness, and in the dirty dishes. It is easy to confuse intrigue with value, and easy to view yourself as the least valuable part of the church.

Mothers need to study their own roles, and begin to see them, not as boring and inconsequential, but as home, the headwaters of missions.

At the very heart of the gospel is sacrifice, and there is perhaps no occupation in the world so intrinsically sacrificial as motherhood. Motherhood is a wonderful opportunity to live the gospel. Jim Elliot famously said, "He is no fool who gives up that which he cannot keep to gain that which he cannot lose." Motherhood provides you with an opportunity to lay down the things that you cannot keep on behalf of the souls that you cannot lose. They are eternal souls, they are your children, they are your mission field.

Faith Makes the Small Offering Great

If you are like me, you may be thinking, "What did I ever give up for them? A desk job? Time at the gym? Extra spending money? My twenty-year-old figure? Some sleep?" Doesn't seem like much when you put it next to the work of some of the great missionaries, people who gave their lives for the gospel.

Think about the feeding of the five thousand when the disciples went out and rounded up the food that was available. It wasn't much. Some loaves. Some fish. Think of some woman pulling her fish out and handing it to one of the disciples. Her offering must have felt small. But the important thing about those loaves and those fishes was not how big they were, but whose hands they were given into. In the hands of the Lord, the offering was sufficient. More than sufficient. Even then, there were leftovers. Given in faith, even a small offering becomes great.

Look at your children in faith, and see how many people will be ministered to by your ministering to them. How many people will your children know in their lives? How many grandchildren are represented in the young faces around your table now?

Gain What You Cannot Lose *in Them*

So, if mothers are strategically situated to impact missions so greatly, why does it feel like so little fruit is coming from our work? I think the answer to this is quite simple: sin—like the sins of discontent, pettiness, selfishness, and resentment. Christians often feel like the right thing to do is to be ashamed about what we have. We hear that quote of Jim Elliot's and think that we ought to sell our homes and move to some place where the lost need the gospel.

But I'd like to challenge you to look at Jim Elliot's quote differently. Giving up what you cannot keep does not mean you need to give up your home so you can go serve somewhere else. It means you need to give up *yourself*. Lay yourself down. Sacrifice yourself here, now. Cheerfully wipe the nose for the fiftieth time today. Make dinner again for the people who don't like green beans. Laugh when a vomiting child thwarts your plans. Lay yourself down for the people here with you, the people who annoy you, the people who get in your way, the people who take up so much of your time that you can't read anymore. Rejoice in them. Sacrifice for them. Gain that which you cannot lose *in them.*

It is easy to think you have a heart for orphans on the other side of the world, but to resent the demands of the children in your living room. You cannot have a heart for the gospel and fussiness about your life at the same time. You will never make any difference *there* if you cannot be at peace *here*. You cannot have a heart for missions without a heart for the people around you. A true love of the gospel overflows and overpowers. It will be in everything you do, however drab, however simple, however repetitive.

God loves little offerings. Given in faith, that plate of PB&Js will feed thousands. Your laundry pile, selflessly tackled daily, will be used in the hands of God to clothe many. Offered with thankfulness, your work at home is only the beginning. Do not think that your work does not matter. In God's hands, your offerings will be broken, and broken, and broken again, until all have eaten and are satisfied. And even then, there will be leftovers.

03 Motherhood Is Application

RACHEL JANKOVIC

If I had to pick one word to describe motherhood, I think that word would be *transformation*.

A busy mother's day produces millions of transformations. Dirty children become clean, hungry children fed, tired children rested. Almost every task a mother performs in the course of a normal day can be considered a transformation. Dirty clothes to clean, unhappy children to peaceful, empty fridge to full. Every day we fight against disorder, filth, starvation, and lawlessness, and some days we almost succeed. And then, while we sleep, everything unravels and we start again in the morning—transformation.

Days of these little cycles add up until one day you see a big transformation. A nursing infant has become a boy on a bicycle, a baby bump has grown into a toddler, and a single car seat has become a backseat loaded with brothers and sisters.

Then there is the kind of transformation that we do— not because we work at it, but because we were created to do it. You eat your lunch, and your body transforms your food into nourishment for a developing baby. But while the physical transformation is miraculous, it is the spiritual cycle of food that is so much more important, and so much less talked about. Christian mothering is a constant cycle of nourishment—both physical and spiritual—that brings transformation.

We Apply What We Believe

In the same way our bodies take the food we eat and make it into something a baby can eat, so our souls take what we believe about God and the gospel and faith and life, and apply it in the places that seem too little for it.

Imagine yourself in your kitchen trying to make dinner for a group of little kids who are tired and should have eaten a half hour ago. Imagine that things are going wrong beyond that—maybe you are out of something you assumed you had, your children are fussing with one another, and your littlest is standing on your feet and pulling on your pant leg. (Bonus points if you are wearing maternity pants and this little person is actually capable of pulling your pants down.) You are hot, you are tired, and you are sick of it.

This is no time for a gospel presentation. There isn't time. There isn't attention. There isn't anyone to lead the discussion around the felt board, because you are still scrambling to figure out dinner.

This isn't a time for a gospel *presentation* because it is a time for a gospel *application*. This is a time to take the grace that God has extended to you, and feed your children with it. This is a time to apply what you believe about God's mercy and kindness and longsuffering towards us, and pour it out to them—in a form they can believe in. Just like a baby crying for a bottle, in un-restful times like these your children need to be fed. What they need is spiritual milk. They need you to feed them, not with a lecture, but with application. Gospel application, even with a toddler on top of your toes, brings transformation.

You Have Everything You Need

Mothering is full of difficult moments. Diapers blow out in stores when you have too much in your cart to just walk out. Kids get sick in cars and you pull over on the side of the road wondering just how much can be done with half a bag of wet wipes. When difficult moments appear, belief is not enough. You must apply what you believe.

The good news is you don't need to graduate from some elite mother's training camp to apply the gospel in your life. You need to believe. Trust God. Give thanks. Laugh. Believe, and that will feed your children. Rest in God, and your children will learn to rest in God. Extend God's kindness to you, to them. Forgive them the way God forgave you. You have everything you need to spiritually nourish your children, because you have Christ.

The gospel is not just something to talk about on Sunday morning while you are in clean clothes and the kids are looking orderly. The gospel is not limited to quiet times and reflective moods. The gospel is something to apply while you are nearly upside down in the back of the car trying to buckle a child up who is playing the kazoo and needs his nose wiped.

God is not above these moments. He is teaching us, and leading us, and refining us, in our different moments. He wants us to apply his beautiful gospel in our actions. He wants to see us feeding our children with the grace that he has given to us.

Mimic the Gospel

Of course, this side of heaven we will not do anything perfectly. Harsh words will be spoken. Patience will wear thin.

Frazzled mothers will act frazzled. And when this happens, our own sinfulness does not detract from the power of the gospel, it illustrates why we need it. Do not use your own mistakes as an excuse to wallow about what a bad mother you are. Repent, seek forgiveness, get it right, and move on. Believe. Be forgiven. Then extend that forgiveness, that belief, and that joy, to your children.

As you go about your daily transformations, set your heart on the truth. Mimic the gospel in what you do. Bring peace, bring order, bring joy, and bring laughter. Bring grace because it was brought to you. Give grace because it was given to you. The gospel is not too big to fit into little situations. It is too big not to.

04 How Eternity Shapes Our Mundane

GLORIA FURMAN

The other day our baby played his first prank.

I was holding him on my hip as I talked with a friend. It was time for us to leave so I instructed him, "We gotta go, Judson. Say 'bye' to Shami."

"Bah bah!" he repeated as he waved his little hand in the air. Then he leaned toward my friend with his lips puckered. "Oh! Look Shami, he wants to kiss you!" Shami was delighted by Judson's show of affection. Giggling, she leaned her cheek toward him to receive a kiss.

My son leaned in for the kiss, then at the last second he turned and planted that kiss squarely on my cheek and laughed. Baby's first prank—I was so proud!

Children grow up so fast, don't they? Not a day goes by when I don't say this to myself or hear it from someone else.

Parental Amnesia

But I don't always live like this is true. I suffer from bouts of parental amnesia.

Parental amnesia is not just where you walk into a room and forget why you're carrying the laundry basket with four dirty coffee mugs in it. That's just normal. Parental amnesia is forgetting about two things: tomorrow and eternity.

First, we forget that, Lord willing, our children will

grow up to be adults. I have a hard time imagining my five-year-old as a 35-year-old or a 65-year-old. Her big goals right now are waiting patiently for her first loose tooth and learning to tell the time. Sometimes I think she'll be five forever.

Second, we forget that our children are more than just potential adults. They are people made in God's image, and they have eternal souls. When the mundane looms larger than eternal life, we forget who God is, who we are, and who our children are.

We tend to forget about tomorrow and eternity when our days are filled with the tyranny of the urgent. Do you ever feel like that ball in the arcade game that ricochets off the walls? Supervise homework while diverting toddlers from swishing their arms in the toilet! Hand down verdicts in Mother's Court about whose toy it really is! No wonder it's hard to keep an eternal perspective.

For me, parental amnesia settles like a fog in the morning hours. If I don't renew my mind through the truths in God's word, then the fog doesn't burn off and let the light of the gospel shine in. By the end of the day, I am lost in a cloud of discouragement that doesn't lift.

It's easy to let our perspective get buried in an avalanche of cotton blends at Mount Laundry. Even so, we must make an effort to remember that our job is more than feeding, bathing, clothing, and educating our children. *Our job is remembering eternity.*

Hope in Christ

The reality of forever reminds us to prioritize eternity in our hopes for our children. But before we extend an eternal perspective to others, we must hope in Christ ourselves. Too often my hope is in my ever-changing circumstances.

I say things like, "I really need the baby to take his nap this morning," which is a fine thing to say and a fine thing to look forward to. But if by lunchtime the nap doesn't happen, and I'm so emotionally wasted by it that it ruins my afternoon . . . then I've probably put more faith in that nap than in the never-changing circumstances of the gospel.

God mercifully intercedes in those moments and shows me that his ways are above my ways. By God's grace, I can resist the temptation to treat my children as interruptions to *my* will for my life. Instead, God enables me to treat my children as precious gifts he is using to shape me into his image according to *his* will for my life.

This morning my daughter ran back upstairs to get her purse before we left the house. By carrying an empty purse, she feels that she is ready to save any abandoned puppies or kittens she comes across. (She has only ever found baby geckos where we live in the desert.) While I wrangled our family circus out the door, I thought about calling after her to just leave the purse behind.

But something made me stop. I was impressed by the thought that just yesterday she was the baby who needed to be cared for in every way. And now she already wants to care for others. Lord willing, someday she'll have bigger responsibilities to help the helpless.

In light of eternity, I want to seize day-to-day opportunities to lift her sights to admire God and image him. My train of thought was interrupted as she skipped over the bottom two steps and landed in the foyer, purse in hand. "I got it!" she breathlessly announced. "Now I can bring home baby animals like Jesus brings home us!"

Sometimes God uses our children to remind us of the eternal perspective that we've forgotten. They grow up so fast, don't they?

05 Desperate, Breathless, Dependent Parenting

RACHEL PIEH JONES

(PART 1 IN THE MOMMY WARS SERIES)

Some people tell me it is brave to raise my kids in Africa. They could get malaria or be bitten by a poisonous snake. They don't have Sunday school class. They can't eat gluten-free foods. Their friends are Muslims. They live far away from cousins, aunts, uncles, and grandparents.

My initial reaction is to say, "Well, I think it is brave to raise kids in America." I know my heart and my soul-shriveling tendency to love the world. I know my kids, and how quickly they can be sucked into the idolatry of a nation whose church is the shopping mall and whose god is the latest iPhone.

But this kneejerk reaction is wrong because it assumes *brave* is the right word to use to describe parenting, whether in Africa or in the United States.

Brave is the wrong word.

Life As Fasting

Living overseas is a form of fasting: fasting from the comforts of a would-be heaven on earth where there are hot showers, dishwashers, clothes dryers, fully stocked grocery stores, and someone else to teach piano lessons. Living overseas is fasting that says: This much, O God, this much, I want to know you. And it says: This much, O God, this much, I want you to be known.[1]

I want to know God deeply, and I want him to be known so much that I will risk scary diseases, fast from my beloved family and worldly comforts, and teach my children to engage with neighbors of differing faiths. But to live and fast like that, to raise my children like that, isn't *brave*.

When I think about mothering my three children who love this steamy, desert nation, I don't feel brave, I feel helplessly, desperately, breathlessly, *dependent*.

Dependent

Any mother, anywhere in the world, could receive a phone call in the next five minutes about a car accident. My child could decide Jesus is an imaginary friend and reject truth. Another could fall into immoral living. There is nothing brave about loving little people who could choose to abandon the things of God. In the face of all these frightening possibilities (and many others), we are tempted to terror and anxiety, until we cling in dependency on the promises of God.

Being dependent isn't just for mothers living in Africa. The only way to parent is with faith that God is able to keep and hold our children. The only way to parent is to be dependent on his sovereign plan and tender care for them. The only way to parent is to be dependent on the strength of the everlasting arms to hold us, to hold our children, and to keep us in perfect peace with our minds stayed on him.

Brave is not the right word for parents. Dependent is.

06 Are You Mom Enough?

RACHEL PIEH JONES
(PART 2 IN THE MOMMY WARS SERIES)

I have spent ten of my twelve mommying years in Africa, so when an American friend mentioned the mommy wars, I had to ask her what that was.

Apparently, as she informed me, there is a perceived mothering battleground where moms pit themselves against each other over topics like feeding babies, choosing schools, eating healthy, disciplining children, and more.

Are You Mom Enough?

Time Magazine recently joined the fray with the cover photo of a young mother breastfeeding her four-year old son under the title, "Are You Mom Enough?"

From this issue of *Time*, from television, from Facebook, from blogs, and from Pinterest the message screamed at moms is this: unless you are fit to run marathons, breastfeed into the preschool years, own a spotless and creatively decorated home, tend a flourishing garden, prepare three home-cooked meals per day, work a high-powered job, *and* give your husband expert, sensual massages before bed, you are not "mom enough."

From my perspective, however, the mommy war is over. Done. Finished. *Kaput.*

And I lost.

I am not mom enough. Never was, never will be.

But I *am* on the frontlines of another war. The battles are raging and the casualties could be my children, my husband, or myself. This war isn't about me being "mom enough." This war is about God being "God enough."

Is God God Enough?

Is God "God enough" when my daughter falls from the roof and the nearest hospital is a two-hour drive and a four-hour flight away? Is God "God enough" when a beloved friend and devoted mother is diagnosed with cancer? Is God "God enough" when loneliness and culture shock creep in like a snake and squeeze my heart? Is God "God enough" to take my best, stained efforts at childrearing and craft something that brings him pleasure? Is God "God enough" to turn little hearts to him, and to hold them there?

Five loaves and two fish fed thousands. A shepherd boy took out a giant. A king who committed adultery and murder was called "a man after God's own heart." A pagan prostitute bore the bloodlines of Jesus. A man dead and buried for days inhaled fresh life. An outcast, stained with a continual flow of blood, was healed with the touch of a tunic. The wind and waves were stilled. The sting of death was vanquished, the curse removed forever.

God always has been, and always will be, God enough. The battle is over, whether or not I believe it, and whether or not I delight in God's enough-ness.

Mom Enough

Somehow, in God's mathematics of grace:

Mom (never enough)
+
God (infinitely enough)
=
Mom enough.

Mom enough to believe and to be called Chosen, Daughter, Righteous, Honored, Heir, Forgiven, Redeemed.

Trusting in God, because of Christ, I will rise from the graveyard of mommy war victims, victorious and filled with resurrection power. Living in his perfect sufficiency, I will live to parent for another day. Never mom enough, but filled with the One who is always enough.

07 The End of the Mommy Wars

CHRISTINE HOOVER

(PART 3 IN THE MOMMY WARS SERIES)

Every other week this spring, I opened my home to a group of new moms to discuss biblical motherhood. Each of them arrived with their babies and baby gear in tow, and with a palpable fear that they were getting it all wrong.

There is an inherent danger in gathering moms in a room: we immediately compare notes regarding our children's milestones, personalities, and sleep habits. Really, though, we are comparing ourselves, wondering if we are good moms.

With the new moms, I addressed this tendency toward comparison on the first day. Until we stop comparing ourselves or telling other moms they should mother our way, I say, we will leave our time together feeling isolated and condemned.

The gospel of Christ holds no place for comparison. We are all equally in need of grace, and we all equally receive it as a gift from God. In regards to mothering, the gospel clearly applies:

- None of us are mom enough.
- Through Christ, God offers us grace in our mothering. He takes our meager efforts and produces spiritual fruit in us and in our children. He is enough.

- He has given us principles in Scripture as a framework for mothering.
- He has also given us the Holy Spirit to *individually* lead and guide us in mothering our *unique* children.

What does this mean for day-in, day-out motherhood?

It means that we are all mothering toward the same goal—that our children know and worship God. Our methods for reaching that goal may vary according to our unique families, circumstances, and the leadership of the Holy Spirit. Will he lead every believer toward the same goal? Yes. Will he lead every believer to the goal in the same way? No. And this is a *very good thing*. Nancy Wilson writes:

> *Because every family is a distinct cultural unit, it is good that our methods differ. God did not intend for us to walk in lockstep with one another. . . . We ought to rejoice in a common commitment to biblical principles and in the variety of methods God's people employ.*[3]

Because of the gospel, mommy wars have no place among believers. After all, at the heart of these wars are pride ("I am more spiritual than that mother because I employ this method and she does not"), competition ("My children are better than hers because I employ this method"), and self-condemnation ("I am not spiritual enough or a good enough mother because I don't employ the method that she does").

To end the mommy wars in the church, we must learn to apply the gospel to our own mothering, and also to the mothering methods of others. When we know God's grace, we stop looking for validation from others for our methods, and we are able to extend grace to others. We celebrate and respect the different gifts and styles of mothering as we move toward a common goal.

These are all the things I said to the new moms in my living room. I pleaded with them earnestly to remember grace, to turn off the chorus of (good) voices on the Internet and (good) books on their shelves, and to focus on the only voice that matters, the quiet whisper of the Holy Spirit in the pages of Scripture.

08 Mommy Wars in the Local Church: A Parable

GLORIA FURMAN

(PART 4 IN THE MOMMY WARS SERIES)

This parable[3] was told to some mothers who engaged in mommy wars and trusted in themselves that they figured it all out, and treated others with contempt.

Two mothers woke up and opened their Bibles to pray, one a perfect mother and the other a not-so-perfect mother. The perfect mother prayed thus: "God, I thank you that I am 'Mom enough,' not like other mothers who have no clue what they're doing, or even like those whose children disobey and don't achieve as much as mine do."

But the not-so-perfect mother prayed, "God, help me, a grace-dependent mother whose faith is so small but whose God is so great!"

Christian and non-Christian mothers alike decry the issue of mother-to-mother destructive criticism. Their voices weigh in by the hundreds of thousands against the mommy wars.

Many women, with cynical derision, claim the mommy wars are more prevalent *inside* the church, and that is because *inside* the church, motherhood-related issues are more likely to be assigned a moral value, creating a game that no mother can win.

Understanding Mommy Wars

Like Rachel (in chapter six), I find these wars to be foreign. In fact, I asked some friends back home in the States to explain how their lives were impacted. We left the U.S. before our oldest was 16 months, before do-it-yourself online stores were generating income for Proverbs 31 hopefuls, before social media sites showcased our God-given creativity with professional cameras, and before organic food was available in major grocery food stores.

Our other two children were born in the Middle East. Here, when someone asks me about my mothering, it is often in the vein of "It takes a village to raise a child, so what village are you from?" There's little competition here, mostly sincere intrigue and concern.

I asked my friends: Are Christian mothers more violent contenders in this culturally-facilitated mommy war? Do the moral values of Christian mothers make us more likely to throw other mothers under the bus *rather than build them up in the gospel?*

Moral and Non-Moral Matters

The Bible does in fact assign moral value to certain parenting practices. Ephesians 6:4 comes to mind, "Do not provoke your children to anger, but bring them up in the discipline and instruction of the Lord." The moral *value* of this parenting practice is indisputable. Our moral *potential* for this parenting practice is also indisputable. We are sinners in need of God's grace!

But most of the outrage against mother-to-mother criticism comes from the assigning of arbitrary moral values to *non-moral* mothering techniques or practices. Take nursing and bottle-feeding for example. I have heard both of these moral judgments: "You nurse your baby? Shame on you." And, "You use bottles? Shame on you."

When we acknowledge the heart idols of competitive mothering we can understand who fired the first shot in the mommy wars. We all did.

Mommy Wars in the Church

Christian mothers must not accept mommy wars in the church. Mommy wars are a contradiction of a community founded on Jesus Christ.

Knowing God's forgiveness, and knowing that we are forgiven sinners, frees us from the very things that spoil our relations with each other. Forgiveness frees Christian mothers from the need to prove anything. It frees us from envy and one-up-mothering. It frees us from the craving for approval and praise that we seek from others. It liberates us to value each other in Christ, and to love our mother-neighbors as ourselves.

In other words, the cross makes possible the fellowship that the mommy wars threaten to tear down.

So-called mommy wars have no place among Christian sisters. Christian mothers are weak and needy for one another. Like the faithful Canaanite mother, we approach the Savior on our knees, saying, "Lord, help me" (Matt. 15:21–28). That is the posture of the needy, Christian mother.

We cherish the shed blood of Jesus Christ who cleanses us from our sin and we live peaceably with one another because of the cross. Moreover, we love to boast all the more gladly of our weaknesses, so that the power of Christ may rest upon us!

We approach the Savior on our knees, there empowered to "put away all malice and all deceit and hypocrisy and envy and all slander" and "consider how to stir up one another to love and good works" (1 Pet. 2:1, Heb. 10:24).

Instead of taking the next shot to slander a mother who does things differently, Jesus gives us the grace we need to adorn the gospel. Jesus gives us the grace to be reverent in behavior, teach what is good, train young women to love their husbands and children, be self-controlled, be pure, work at home, be kind, and be submissive to our own husbands (Titus 2).

09 Mommy Wars Are Spiritual Wars

CAROLYN MCCULLEY

(PART 5 IN THE MOMMY WARS SERIES)

As a part of American jargon, the mommy wars have raged for more than 20 years. The term was coined in the late 1980s by *Child* magazine to describe the tension that existed between working and stay-at-home mothers. Since then, numerous books and articles have been published about the so-called mommy wars, feeding the talk show circuit and fueling blogosphere brushfires.

Compared to the mommy wars, cultural ambivalence about motherhood has a much longer history. Allow me a moment for a quick overview.

Shortly after our nation was founded, motherhood hit a high note. As historian Glenna Matthews writes, this new political experiment needed mothers:

> *There were no precedents for a republic on the scale of the United States. Many people believed that the new nation would require the support of a uniquely public-spirited citizenry. If citizens must learn to place a high value on the public interest, this was a lesson they would need to begin in childhood. Thus the home became crucial to the success of the nation and women—whose education began to be taken much more seriously than ever before— gained the role of "Republican Mother."* [4]

Soon the Republican Motherhood concept began to spill out of the home into the public square as women organized benevolent agencies to combat drunkenness, slavery, gambling, and other problems of the age.

Mommy Wars, Darwinism, and Margaret Sanger

Republican Motherhood met its demise when Charles Darwin released his 1859 publication, *On the Origin of Species*. Darwin viewed women as lesser beings in the system of evolution. His ideas were immediately embraced by Social Darwinists, who claimed that since men had always fought for survival in the world, they were honed by competition and natural selection. In comparison, women were sheltered from this process because they were at home with the children—thus, they "evolved" more slowly.

With motherhood thus devalued, children became the next targets. Margaret Sanger, who founded what later became Planned Parenthood, believed that most evils stemmed from large families. As she wrote in her 1920 book, *Woman and the New Race*, "the most merciful thing that a large family does to one of its infant members is to kill it."

Sanger was a vocal proponent of eugenics—the theory of race improvement that was the cornerstone of Nazi Germany. Her monthly magazine, *Woman Rebel*, was published under the slogan, "No gods; no masters!" For Sanger, the birth control movement was founded on two goals: limiting the reproduction of the "unfit" and challenging Christian teaching by creating a "new morality." She campaigned against women who "with staggering rapidity" were breeding "those numberless, undesired children who become the clogs and the destroyers of civilization."

Sanger's scorched-earth writing left no one guessing

about her views. She confidently predicted a future that never materialized.

> When motherhood becomes the fruit of a deep yearning, not the result of ignorance or accident, its children will become the foundation of a new race. There will be no killing of babies in the womb by abortion, nor through neglect in foundling homes, nor will there be infanticide. . . . Child slavery, prostitution, feeblemindedness, physical deterioration, hunger, oppression and war will disappear from the earth. . . . When the womb becomes fruitful through the desire of an aspiring love, another Newton will come forth to unlock further the secrets of the earth and the stars. There will come a Plato who will be understood, a Socrates who will drink no hemlock, and a Jesus who will not die upon the cross.[5]

On the contrary, there is *no* hope for "child slavery, prostitution, feeblemindedness, physical deterioration, hunger, oppression and war to disappear from the earth" if the Father's righteous anger against these terrible sins is not satisfied! Where would justice be in the universe if such sins went overlooked? There is no hope of a new heavens and a new earth, free from the effects of the Fall, without the atonement of our sinless Savior. There is no hope for mercy to triumph over judgment unless it be found at the foot of that cross. Our only hope is the cross!

Therefore, the real mommy wars are not against other people and their parenting styles, nor even against Darwin, Sanger or those who promote similar ideologies. As Ephesians 6:12 says, "we do not wrestle against flesh and blood, but against the rulers, against the authorities, against the cosmic powers over this present darkness, against the spiritual forces of evil in the heavenly places." *The real mommy wars are spiritual.* And they began with the very first mother, Eve.

The First Mommy War and You

Eve's initial assignment, along with her husband Adam, was to be "fruitful and multiply and fill the earth" (Gen. 1:28). But after the Fall, childbearing became painful and opposed. When the LORD God cursed the serpent that deceived Eve, he said, "I will put enmity between you and the woman, and between your offspring and her offspring; he shall bruise your head, and you shall bruise his heel" (Gen. 3:15).

Ever since, Satan has labored to destroy the offspring of those who are made in the image of God. *The real mommy wars are not against flesh and blood, but against the one who seeks to destroy the next generation of those who would rise up to praise God.*

You may be a mother in the thick of rearing children right now. Perhaps it took you several attempts to read this chapter, thanks to the constant interruptions of young children. Your daily life may consist of dozens of repetitive tasks that feel mundane and irrelevant. This is absolutely not true! *You are engaged in spiritual warfare.* You are standing against those who believe heinous lies, like "the most merciful thing that a large family does to one of its infant members is to kill it." By bearing and nurturing life, you are reflecting the life-giving characteristics of our holy God. Made in his image, you are reflecting him when you care for the lives he has created.

This truth applies to those of us who are childless, too. Whether you are not yet married, or married but not yet pregnant, or past the age of bearing children—whatever season of life you are in, you are still part of the great community of believers who are called to witness to the majesty of God: "One generation shall commend your works to another, and shall declare your mighty acts" (Ps. 145:4).

It may be quite bitter not to have children of your own, but I ask you to be strategic about the battle. Where can you stand against the devil's schemes and invest in the children God has already put in your life? Where can you reach out? So many hurting children exist and so many are being discarded.

The real mommy wars need every believing woman to enlist. The battle is more significant and more costly than we can perceive.

10 A Pregnant Woman's Defense Against the Schemes of the Devil

GLORIA FURMAN

(THE FINAL PART OF THE MOMMY WARS SERIES)

If you are a pregnant mom, perhaps with your first baby, you may be reading these six chapters about mommy wars and shaking your head. As if you didn't have enough on your mind already!

In the chaos of battles over things like bottle-feeding, co-sleeping, and baby wearing, Carolyn has pointed out how the real mommy wars are primarily spiritual battles (see chapter nine). The real battles are not against other moms who have different mothering preferences, but against our adversary the devil, who prowls around like a roaring lion seeking someone to devour (1 Pet. 5:8).

God has provided protection for the pregnant woman against the schemes of the devil. *The armor of God comes in maternity sizes.*

For the next 42 weeks (or less) you have a unique opportunity to be strong in the Lord and in the strength of his might (Eph. 6:10). Even when you're wearing support hosiery and your center of gravity has shifted to your navel.

When a pregnant woman wears the armor of God, her endurance is based on "the immeasurable greatness of his power toward us who believe, according to the working of his great might" (Eph. 1:19).

When Paul said he could do "all things through Christ

who strengthens me" he wasn't only talking about throwing a baseball or lifting weights (Phil. 4:13). He was talking about learning contentment in the permanent circumstance of God's sovereign goodness toward him. The power of God toward you is "according to the riches of his glory that he may grant you to be strengthened with power through his Spirit in your inner being" (Eph. 3:16).

Pregnant ladies, you can do all things through Christ who strengthens you, when you ground your faith in God's sovereign goodness as the basis for your contentment. I know it is hard to be content when you're weary, when your heart is distracted with fear for your baby, and when your emotions careen out of control. But God's power is more than adequate for these things; his immeasurable greatness of power can overwhelm every scheme the devil devises to steal your joy in God.

The Armor of God Fits Over Maternity Elastic

Scripture exhorts us to "put on the whole armor of God, that you may be able to stand against the schemes of the devil" (Eph. 6:11). Even when the only pants that currently fit you are held up on your hips by a yard of elastic, the armor of God still fits you, and you should wear it. When you put on the armor of God, you can stand firm against the schemes of the devil as he tries to deceive you and unsettle your faith (Eph. 4:14).

Here are a few style tips for pregnant ladies to remember about the armor of God.

Belt

The "belt of truth" encircles you with the confident protection of knowing who God is, what Christ has done for you, and who you are in light of your being "in Christ" through faith in him. Through whatever means necessary, you must take pains to hold up this belt of truth around you. Engage in spiritual disciplines, meditate on God's word, commit Scripture to memory, and actively pursue fellowship with other women who will remind you of God's truth.

Breastplate

The "breastplate of righteousness" is one-size-fits-all-who-believe. The righteousness of Jesus Christ is imputed by faith to sinners who deserve death and judgment for their sins. We understand that by "the one man's disobedience the many were made sinners, so by the one man's obedience the many will be made righteous" (Rom. 5:19).

Pregnant sister, you will be tempted by the adversary to put forward your own righteousness as a front when you're feeling insecure. The devil will try to build insecurity about your pregnancy, your prenatal care, your birth plan, and even your mothering potential. Guard yourself against the temptation to comfort yourself with self-righteous pats on the back. Arm yourself with Jesus's warning against parading your righteousness before others to gain admiration and respect from them (Matt. 6:1).

As you put on the breastplate of Christ's righteousness, you can stand firm against the devil's lies of inadequacy and failure. Wear the breastplate of righteousness, Martin Luther-style:

> So when the devil throws your sins in your face and declares that you deserve death and hell, tell him this: "I admit that I deserve death and hell, what of it? For I know One who suffered and made satisfaction on my behalf. His name is Jesus Christ, Son of God, and where He is there I shall be also!"

Shoes

The shoes of the armor of God not only fit you, but they make your feet move. You know how special this is when you're already fatigued by ten o'clock in the morning and you can watch your feet widening with every pregnancy. "As shoes for your feet . . . put on the readiness given by the gospel of peace" (Eph. 6:15).

The gospel of peace provides readiness by giving you the reason and the power to go wherever Christ leads you for his sake. The gospel empowers you to go into the fray of the mommy wars and announce to the contenders the victory of the cross, "Grace to you and peace from God our Father and the Lord Jesus Christ!"

Shield

The "shield of faith" is for your protection all day and into the sleepless nights. "In all circumstances take up the shield of faith, with which you can extinguish all the flaming darts of the evil one" (Eph. 6:16). It doesn't matter if your faith is as small as a mustard seed or as small as the hCG hormones circulating through your blood. What matters is the greatness of the One in whom you have placed your faith.

As you get excited about the upcoming birth of your child, rejoice most of all in him who has caused you to be born again to a living hope through the resurrection of Jesus Christ (1 Pet. 1:3, 23). When you take up the shield of faith and watch as the devil's flaming darts implode into little puffs of smoke, give thanks to God: "But thanks be to God, who gives us the victory through our Lord Jesus Christ" (1 Cor. 15:57).

Sword

In the weakness of your back pain, and in the vulnerability of your nausea, remember your hope of salvation in Christ. Rely on Scripture, your offensive weapon against the enemy. "Take the helmet of salvation, and the sword of the Spirit, which is the word of God" (Eph. 6:17).

Don't just *not* believe the lies of the devil, but speak God's truth to yourself. Don't just *not* dwell on your bloated appearance and spider veins, but talk to yourself of the beauty of Christ's sacrificial love and how he gave his body up for us all. Delight in God's grace as you let your body serve the life of another.

Pray

Finally, purpose your mind, will, and emotions to submit to God's good plan to glorify himself in all things. Be "praying at all times in the Spirit, with all prayer and supplication. To that end keep alert with all perseverance, making supplication for all the saints" (Eph. 6:18).

This is the power of God in a pregnant woman whose hope is in the victory of Christ Jesus over the schemes of the devil.

11 The Everyday Question of Motherhood

CHRISTINE HOOVER

As mothers, we face many challenging questions. Will I teach my children the gospel? Will I share the truth of Scripture with them? Will I raise my children to love God?

But there is another constant question of motherhood that is more subtle, more everyday, more hideable. At the center is one question: *Will I sacrifice?*

The Everyday Question isn't answered one time, with the birth of a child, with the planning of school, or with the decision to discipline. This question—*Will I sacrifice?*—is answered everyday.

It's answered when a child wakes early with a need, interrupting my quiet hour alone with the Lord. It's answered when a sick child keeps me from worship and adult interaction at church on Sunday morning. It's answered when I am emotionally spent, but a child's behavior requires my patient, purposeful response. It's answered as I systematically teach my special-needs son how to interact with others.

In motherhood, the Everyday Question is answered every time a child's concern or need must come before my own. (And as every mother knows, this is most of the time.)

Too often, I attend to necessary tasks—leaving the

stove to help with pant buttons, putting down the phone to search for a beloved toy, excusing myself from a conversation at church to take tired children home for a nap—while my heart grumbles: "If I just had one moment to complete a task or have an adult conversation without an interruption."

The Everyday Question asks not just about my duties, but also about my attitude. Will I joyfully pour out my life as a fragrant offering before the Lord for the benefit of my children? Will I serve my children out of obligation and duty, or will I serve out of the joy of serving God himself? Will I die to myself so that I might live to God in the specific calling he has given me as a mom?

The Everyday Question must be answered *everyday*. Because motherhood is not so much the big, dramatic acts of sacrifice, but the little, everyday, unseen ones. Because we can have a clean house and obedient children and not sacrifice. Because we are so easily deceived to think we can live for ourselves and be faithful to God in our ministry as moms.

Jesus said that those who live for themselves will have an unfulfilling life, but those who lose for their lives for his sake will *really experience life*. As parents, our self-death for Christ's sake not only produces fruit in our own hearts, but also produces fruit in the hearts of our children, fruit that grows by the power of God. Let us choose to joyfully give of ourselves for our children.

Everyday.

"For we who live are always being given over to death for Jesus' sake, so that the life of Jesus also may be manifested in our mortal flesh" (2 Cor. 4:11).

"For the love of Christ controls us, because we have concluded this: that one has died for all, therefore all have died; and he died for all, that those who live might no longer live for themselves but for him who for their sake died and was raised" (2 Cor. 5:14–15).

12 A Treasure Greater Than Our Homes

CHRISTINE HOOVER

The home exists for Christ. Our marriages, our children, our physical spaces, are all means of joyful response to him. Through our homes, we treasure Christ and show others how to treasure him also (Titus 2:3–5; Prov. 31:10–31).

Too often, however, we treasure our homes more than we treasure Christ. As a result, what he has given as a blessing and an avenue of sanctification becomes a means of achievement or accomplishment. Our well-behaved children or our organizational abilities become displays of our value and righteousness. Our homes become a matter of pride, self-elevation, or comparison. We cling to our treasure, thinking that the home is under our control, that it's ours to possess, that we have created and cultivated something special.

This temptation to treasure the home is especially intense on good days, when our children are playing nicely together, when we're unified with our spouse, or when the house is bright and clean and everything is in order.

But on bad days? When a child throws a fit or disrespects another adult? When the dishwasher leaks all over the kitchen floor or an appointment is forgotten? When a harsh word is spoken or priorities are shoved aside? When life is thrown off-kilter, or when our communication gets crisscrossed?

When the home is the treasure above Christ, and our value is entwined with the circumstances of the home, the bad days are unsettling, even devastating.

On the bad days, we recognize the home acting similarly to the Law:

- Our treasure, the home, speaks urgent, ever-changing, and unending demands for perfection that can never be fulfilled (Gal. 3:10).
- Our treasure, the home, causes us to value and conform to what pleases others or earns their respect, rather than what pleases God (Col. 2:20–22).
- Our treasure, the home, with its perfectionistic, image-maintaining urgencies, cannot bring life to our hearts and our families (Gal. 3:21).

If we treasure our homes as our righteousness, we subtly teach our children that behavior matters more than the attitudes of the heart. We teach them that a clean home matters more than relationships, or that we must cling to and control the things we love rather than trust God with them.

The good news is that even when we treasure our homes more than we treasure Christ, our failings act as a tutor to bring us to Christ, the true Treasure, and to show us that we are incapable of righteousness apart from him (Gal. 3:21–26). We recognize in our failings that we need something apart from ourselves to make a home as God intended—and that something is the grace and power of Christ.

When Christ is our treasure, our homes consist of love, grace, and utter dependence on the Holy Spirit. We don't chase self-righteousness, and we don't cling to treasures that can be lost. We cling tightly to the only Treasure that cannot be stolen or tarnished, Christ himself.

13 Femininity: June Cleaver, Clair Huxtable, or the Valiant Woman?

TRILLIA NEWBELL

One of my role models growing up was Oprah Winfrey. I dreamed of being like her one day. After high school, I went to college and did everything I could to be successful. I made good grades, took internships, studied abroad, and got into law school. Then something odd happened. I began to sense God calling me to be a wife and mother.

Yikes!

I remember sharing my desire to be a wife and mother with a research professor. The idea was not well received. Apparently I was forfeiting all that the Civil Rights leaders had worked so hard for me to be able to do as a black woman. Without an understanding of how the Lord can change hearts and minds, I can easily see how my decision not to go to law school could appear foolish.

I felt pressure from the world to be "successful," but I also felt the desire to be a mother. Where could I look for guidance?

June Cleaver?

As God began to change my heart, I started to wonder what the application of this newfound desire for motherhood looked like. I was convinced that motherhood was a high calling, but did that mean I was called to be a stay-at-home mother? Thankfully I also had a husband to help me wade through these issues, and we came to conclude: *yes* and *no*.

That doesn't sound like much of a conclusion. But yes, God calls women to pay close attention to their homes. The woman who is oriented to her home is even called wise. "The wisest of women builds her house, but folly with her own hands tears it down" (Prov. 14:1). The home matters, and throughout Scripture God makes reference to the home and its importance (Prov. 24:3; 15:6; 3:33; Titus 2:5).

Yet are all mothers called to be June Cleaver? You remember the fictional character of the show *Leave it to Beaver*. *The New York Times* remembers June's character (played by Barbara Billingsley) as a woman who wore pearls and high heels at home and helped her family get out of jams. June baked a steady supply of cookies, and used "motherly intuition to sound the alarm about incipient trouble." June was joyful, agreeable, and content in her role. There is much to commend in her character.

But I wonder if June was not also the product of a particular 1950s American milieu. She was at home in her white suburban neighborhood. She served her family well, but she wasn't always a good example of strength, initiative, or courage. Her activity in the community was limited to social events like weddings and school fundraisers. June was ideal only in part.

Clair Huxtable?

In contrast, another American icon busied her life around caring for her family and work: Clair Huxtable.

Clair (played by Phylicia Rashād) was witty and tough. She was a lawyer and the mother of five children on *The Cosby Show*. Clair cared for her husband and listened to her children. And in 2004, her character was named "Best

TV Mom" by a poll conducted by the Opinion Research Corporation.

But I wonder if Clair was the product of 1980s feminism? Clair was aggressive, and at times bossy. The saying, "If momma ain't happy, ain't nobody happy," applied to the Huxtable household. When the kids stepped out of line or didn't meet her standards, it was judgment time (check out "The Night of the Wretched," season 6, episode 22, for a good example).

Though she cared deeply for her husband, she often treated him like a child, not trusting him as he ventured into his many household projects. She worked hard for her family, which is commendable, but like June Cleaver, her fictional character falls short of ideal.

The Valiant Woman

From all appearances, June and Clair loved their homes, their husbands, and their children. But there is another woman who provides a better role model for us. If we want to gain a biblical vision for the ideal woman, we should look at the wise words of King Lemuel's mother in Proverbs 31.

I know that many people are tired of the Proverbs 31 woman and are cringing at that subtitle. But as Paul reminds us, "*All* Scripture is breathed out by God and profitable for teaching, for reproof, for correction, and for training in righteousness, that the man of God may be complete, equipped for every good work" (2 Tim. 3:16–17). God says his words are useful for the man of God and for the woman of God. That means that even if the "excellent wife" has been overused, his word still stands true. The Proverbs 31 woman is an ideal woman because she teaches us wisdom.

The Proverbs 31 woman, the "excellent wife," is noble.

She is respectful to her husband, she is trustworthy and kind, she is brave, she takes initiative, she works with her hands, she works inside and outside of the home, she is wise and respected. She is generous and thoughtful. She enjoys her children. Her children bless her. She is valiant.

A Radical Change of Heart

Most importantly, the valiant woman fears the Lord (Prov. 31:30). This is what God desires for us. God wants our hearts. He wants to give us new hearts and new purposes (Ezek. 36:26–28). When he changes us, he changes us to the core. God's desire is that we love him with all our hearts and love our neighbors as ourselves (my closest neighbors being my husband and children).

The radical change in my heart calls for a radical change in my pursuits, which brings me back to the decision my husband and I had to face. I personally could not be Clair and pursue my law degree while still trying to care for my husband, care for my home, and serve my children. Yet I couldn't be June: I work part-time, I'm not ironing my husband's underpants, and when I wake up I have a fight that the fictional character didn't have. I fight my selfish flesh by the word of God and through his grace. I need to look to God's word for direction, not to the world.

A Miracle Only God Could Do

I didn't first jump at the thought of having children, and I definitely didn't jump at the idea of femininity as defined by Scripture. It took time for God to reveal his will and heart to me in the Scriptures. Now in marriage, because God has been so very gracious to me, I can and do submit. I love to be home with my children, and this is a miracle that only God could do in my heart. I had to fight (and continue to fight) the world—not only feminist thoughts, but a culture that would say I sold out.

With God's help, I can be a valiant woman who wields God's word in the fight against feminism, against traditionalism, and against the cultural pressures every mother must face today.

14 The Amazing Calling of Motherhood

TRILLIA NEWBELL

The other morning I woke up while my children were still sleeping and began to pray. I started thinking about my identity. *Who am I?* As I settled into my prayer time, I began to rejoice at the thought that I am a mother. It is part of who I am. To my children, it is my name: Mom.

The modern mom doesn't always like to be identified as a mother. We have names and identities of much greater significance. Even the Christian mommy would prefer to keep her mom identity in check. "I am a Christian first and foremost," we might say, which is true and good. First and foremost, we are united to Christ. He has redeemed us and therefore our identities are wrapped up in his righteousness. But this doesn't mean we must deny the significance of being a mother.

Rather than shed the title of mother, we must see the true significance of this name. One great example of a mother's significance can be found in the biblical account of Timothy. Timothy was the son of a believing Jewish mother and an unbelieving Greek father (Acts 16:1–2). And we get some crucial information about his mother, Eunice.

Timothy was a young pastor and Paul's child in the faith (1 Tim. 1:2). Paul loved Timothy for his faithfulness to the sacred texts and for his friendship (2 Tim. 3:15, 10–11). When everyone abandoned Paul during his imprisonment in Rome, Timothy remained faithful to Paul through prayers and tears (2 Tim. 1:3–5). Paul was greatly affected by the ministry and love of his apprentice. And Paul attributes Timothy's faith and character to his mother's and his grandmother's faithful witness.

Paul references the legacy of these women in two places. First, we see their influence when Paul thanks God for Timothy and his faith. He reminds him that his sincere faith dwelt first in his grandmother Lois, and then his mother Eunice, and "now, I am sure, dwells in you as well" (2 Tim. 1:5). Later, Paul encourages Timothy to stay strong in the word, not being deceived under the persecution that surely comes from those who follow Christ (2 Tim. 3:12–14). Here again Paul reminds Timothy of the word that he learned and firmly believed from a young age, "from childhood" (2 Tim. 3:15).

Moms, Timothy's story is very significant. Eunice and Lois invested in Timothy to teach him about God. The gospel was passed on to Timothy and from Timothy to other generations. More importantly, Timothy now enjoys the benefits of being with Christ, forever.

God has called us, Moms, to train up our children in the way they should go (Prov. 22:6). This is Great Commission work. We don't need to shed out titles as moms, we leverage our titles for what they mean for the glory of Christ. We can embrace our roles without grumbling and with the full assurance of God's sovereign goodness. God promises that as we shine light into this world (and that includes into our kids) we will know that our labor was not in vain (Phil. 2:12–16).

On this side of heaven we may never know the significance of our mothering, but we know Lois's and Eunice's. As a result of their faithfulness to embrace their role in the life of one little boy named Timothy, generations of sinners have been saved.

15 Grace Greater Than All Our Worries

CHRISTINA FOX

"Mommy, what's the matter?"

My son can sense it. The tension and worry that saturates my heart oozes from my presence. "I just have so much on my mind. I forgot to do something, that's all," I replied.

But that's not all. I say it like it's not a big deal. But from the mouth of a child, his question reminds me that I shouldn't feel this way. This burden I'm carrying on my shoulders seems to get heavier with each new day. Lately, my to-do lists have to-do lists.

With a hectic, busy life, I'm afraid I'll forget something crucial and important. I worry that if I don't do *it* (and there's always an *it*), then no one else will. So I try to keep everything under my control. I'm constantly reminding myself of what I have to do. "I can't forget this. . ." "I better do that first thing tomorrow." "It would be bad if I didn't do this. . ." I focus on all the "what ifs," and the worry consumes me. My child can see it because it's etched across my face.

Yet I am fooling myself. I'm not really in control of anything. I could write a thousand to-do lists, and it wouldn't matter. God is in control, not me. I've been bitten by a serpent-shaped lie that says I can orchestrate, plan, and execute all the details of my life. The lie then produces fear when the reality crashes in that I actually can't do it at all.

Rather than getting control of all that I fear, fear has gotten control of me.

Trust vs. Worry

This desire to control our lives is common among mothers. We voice our worries to each other, talk about our stresses, and strategize how to make our lives smooth and problem-free. Worry is an "acceptable sin" that joins many conversations, play dates, and texts. Sometimes we even encourage worry among one another, attempting to out-do each other to see whose life is most worrisome and hectic. It seems so normal and commonplace, after all. I mean, what mother doesn't worry? And if she didn't, wouldn't there be something wrong with her?

Jesus calls us to a different kind of life, one that's contrary to the world. He calls us to a life of trust (Matt. 6:25–34). Trust is the opposite of worry. It requires that we believe all that God has told us about himself. It requires that we believe he is better than everything else. It requires that we trust in his character, his goodness, and his grace (Ps. 9:10). It requires that we look back to all the ways he has provided for and strengthened us in the past. We know what he has said, and therefore we have the confidence in what he will do in the future. Trusting God requires that we believe he cares for us, and that we keep our eyes on him, not on our circumstances (1 Pet. 5:7).

Remembering His Grace

The Israelites were told over and over in Scripture to look back at how God delivered them from slavery in Egypt. They were to remember his wonders at the Red Sea, his provisions in the desert, and how his rescue brought them into the Promised Land. In annual feasts they were to celebrate what God had done for them and instruct their children about God's faithfulness. But too often, they failed to remember. They turned away from trust in God and relied instead on themselves and the culture around them.

We are also called to remember God's grace in our lives. When worries creep in, when the cares of this life weigh us down, when everything seems out of control, we must remember all that God has done, and all that he continues to do. We must remember our own story of deliverance from sin. We must remember the lengths God went to—and continues to go to—in rescuing us from slavery through the shed blood of his Son at the cross. We must remember where God decisively demonstrated his love (Rom. 5:8). If he would sacrifice his own Son to save us, how will he not also with him graciously give us all things (Rom. 8:32)?

If he saved us from our greatest fear—eternal separation from him—how can he not carry us through all our fears today? If Christ conquered death when he rose triumphantly from the grave, how can he not also resurrect our joy from the pit of worry and despair?

Grace for Today and Every Tomorrow

Like the Israelites, we also forget and stumble, but the cross is there to remind us of the gospel of grace. Just as the Israelites had to look to the bronze serpent for healing in the wilderness, we need to look to Christ. Looking to the cross and remembering the gospel frees us from the burdens that weigh us down. It pulls us away from our inward focus, away from our efforts to control life, and focuses us back to the one who already accomplished it all.

When Jesus spoke the words, "It is finished," he shut the door on our efforts to control our life. He put an end to all our strivings to get everything right in our own strength. And he opened the door to freedom from sin, to a forever rest, and to a peace that passes all understanding.

This life provides plenty of reasons to worry. But God gives us more reasons to trust. God has been more than faithful in the past. Because he sent Jesus to rescue us from our sin, we can trust him with all our worries and fears, today and tomorrow. When life's unexpected challenges and overwhelming tasks tempt us to worry, when our to-do list gets long and sleep evades us, let us look to the cross and believe.

16 The Most Frightening Prayer I Could Pray for My Children

CHRISTINA FOX

The most frightening prayer I could pray for my children is the one they need the most.

I always pray about their behavior, their health, their progress in school, and their friendships. I also pray about their future and their jobs. I pray that my boys will marry "nice Christian girls." But to be honest, when I pray for my children, it is easiest to ask that their lives be smooth, stress-free, comfortable, easy, and free of pain and grief.

When It Gets Uncomfortable

Yet when I reflect on my own life and look back on my faith journey, I see all the challenges and trials I have faced along the way, and all the good that God accomplished through them. I see the heartaches I've endured and the suffering that brought me to my knees. I also see the sins I've struggled with and the idols God graciously stripped from my hands. I see how God used all those valleys and painful circumstances to draw me closer to him, to refine me, and to teach me to rely on him.

Trials have been the most important events in my life, but it's not easy to ask for trials for my children. It is hard to ask that God reveal their sin to them, that they see their need for a Savior, that they are broken over their corruption and truly learn to cling to the gospel.

That kind of prayer is uncomfortable.

The Path to More of Him

Praying for challenges means my children have to dig through rocky terrain like I've experienced before. They will have to walk through their own stories of sin and repentance, and learn what it means to have empty hands. What's frightening for me as a mom is to realize that their lives will not be smooth, comfortable, or safe—not if they will learn most deeply what it means to rely on God. My children may have to endure great trials, walk through dark valleys, and experience great sorrow. Those children could be God's pathway to giving them more of himself.

I don't want my children to treat God like a vending machine or a fire insurance policy. I want them to have a passionate love for God that is alive and outgoing, bowing to his supremacy and anchored gladly in his gospel. I want them to love God's word and hold to it firmly in times of uncertainty. I want them to show Jesus to the world.

Nothing More Important

But first, my children have to see that they have sinned against a holy God and that it is only through the grace and sacrifice of his Son that they can be forgiven. Jesus said that those who have been forgiven little will love little (Luke 7:47). My children need to know what that means. They must see the utter depths of their sinfulness. They must understand that without Jesus, they are without hope. They must trust in Jesus as their only source of hope and righteousness. Only as they acknowledge their need for him and his forgiveness will they grow to love God in the way I most want for them.

This path will likely be hard for my children, and praying for this path is frightening for a mother, but there really is nothing more important. . . . *Father, give my children more of you.*

17 It's Good to Be a Jar of Clay

TRILLIA NEWBELL

Clay jars are delicate. They crack easily, even though they seem durable.

On one hand, clay jars are refined by fire. The kiln furnace carries the clay from an unfinished product to a household amenity. But once completed, the slightest nudge off the table can send a jar plummeting to its demise. The durability is deceiving. The thick porcelain is more delicate than it appears. No wonder the Bible often describes people as jars of clay. We are like potter's vessels, waiting to be broken into millions of tiny pieces (Ps 31:12; Isa. 30:14). We are weak. We get tired and weary. We grow old and frail.

As a mom of small children, I am faced daily with my weakness. Often it's in the form of tiredness and impatience. Motherhood can be tiring, but my children are not at fault for my weakness. They are a great joy and blessing. My tiredness reminds me that I am a part of a fallen world. It makes me feel how badly I need a Savior. A scenario that has played out in my home looks like this: I'm tired, yet in my pride I resist rest. (After all, there's so much to do!) But then this 'tiredness without rest' can lead to impatience with my loved ones.

Embracing the Unlikely Asset

What if I just embrace the fact that I'm a clay jar? What if I don't ignore the fact that as a human I really do get tired sometimes? What if I gain a biblical understanding of what it means to be weak? In God's economy, our weakness is one of our greatest assets. But isn't this hard to believe? It's hard to believe that weakness can be for our good. But what weakness does—like nothing else can—is draw our attention to the One who never grows tired or weary (Isa. 40:28).

Trying harder in our own power doesn't solve our weakness. If anything, it exposes more of our weakness. My self-exertion typically leaves me depleted and empty of joy. Jonathan Parnell writes: "Embracing weakness brings more peace because we realize afresh that God loves us by his grace, not because we are strong. Our joy doesn't rest in our ability, but in the approval God gives us in Christ, the one in whom he chose us before the ages began, according to his own purpose and grace (2 Tim. 1:9)."[6]

This brings joy to a weak and weary mom! God loves you as you are. He didn't call you to himself while you were strong, but while you were weak (1 Cor. 1:27). It was while we were still weak, that Christ died for the ungodly (Rom. 5:6).

Walking with Confidence

That is the great purpose behind why we are called jars of clay. It is to show the surpassing power belongs to God and not to us (2 Cor. 4:7). We are weak, we are frail, we are lame—and yet, we are chosen. We are loved. "God chose what is low and despised in the world, even things that are not, to bring to nothing things that are, so that no human being might boast in the presence of God" (1 Cor.

1:28–29).

Our only boast is in Jesus our Lord who is our wisdom and righteousness, sanctification and redemption (verse 30). He is our perfect righteousness, who not only meets us in our weakness, but covers our every sin by his blood.

Moms, we can walk in our weakness. We can boast in our weakness and confess our need for Jesus. Ironically, this gives us the right kind of confidence. We don't have to walk with a limp, focused on ourselves. We walk confidently, not in our ability, but in the ability of our Savior. We walk confidently, not in our strength, but in his. It is good to be a jar of clay.

18 The Real Life of the Pro-Life Home

RACHEL JANKOVIC

I couldn't be more angered by abortion. So when I first started seeing things about Kermit Gosnell and his grisly crimes, I skipped right over it. Maybe you did the same. What can we possibly do about it? And how can reading about the horror of what happened in that "clinic" help us be any more faithful in our own lives?

But when I finally did read a bit about this story, I found myself surprisingly challenged and encouraged, and here is why. The Gosnell situation shines light on the darkness of abortion in a way that nothing else has in a long time. Stories like this one make me realize that I am just far enough away from the reality of abortion to forget to fight it. I need this kind of reminder. Let me try to explain.

Feeding the Volcano of Self

Abortion in our country is not a standalone movement, brought about by women who somehow haven't heard of adoption. Abortion is a dark crisis of choice served up to millions of women every year, courtesy of our cultural religion of self-fulfillment. It is the bloody path taken by many women who feel that they really "have no choice" (at least if they are going to finish law school, if they are going to have a career, if they are going to be slim in their bikinis in time for spring break). Everyone acts like abortion is sad but necessary. But the truth is that abortion is the sacrifice required by our religion of selfishness.

In some ancient pagan religions, the volcano periodically required worshippers throw in a virgin. She would have no choice, and sometimes even she could understand that. The god had to be fed. Abortion fills that place for us today. Our god is a stupid volcano of selfish desire, sexual "liberty," freedom from God's law, and refusal to accept responsibility for another. This god requires a sacrifice, and so we offer it the unborn and their tragically confused mothers.

The Gosnell case has forced people to see what it is like to die in the volcano—how long it takes on the way down before you die, what the body looks like afterwards, what it smells like, and how it feels to stand on the edge in fear.

The True Sacrifice

So while the pro-life movement absolutely needs to be working hard to save the virgins from the brink of the volcano, we need to understand that it is not the brink that brings about the crisis. The crisis is made by the worship happening further down the mountainside. The people who are busy promising us that there will be no break in easy access to abortion don't care about the victims. They are promising that to each other—to men who want sexual pleasure but can't be bothered with fatherhood, to women who want to be desired and consumed like playthings without ever seeming used. Our god will continue to be appeased. We will ensure that it stays satisfied. We will ensure that we have a steady supply of the unborn to feed it—because if we run out of infants, we would have to go in ourselves. We would actually have to sacrifice ourselves for others.

So here is our culture—deeply involved in the worship of freedom, and this worship requires a death sacrifice. It requires blood. It is a sacrifice of death, from the dying, in the name of life. But we are Christians! We are not on that altar! We place our lives on the altar to the Living God. We are not required to sacrifice with death, but with life. Jesus Christ was our blood sacrifice who rose from the dead, ascended into heaven, and now sits with God the Father.

Choosing Life in the Big and Small

Romans 12:1 says, "I appeal to you therefore, brothers, by the mercies of God, to present your bodies as a *living sacrifice*, holy and acceptable to God, which is your spiritual worship."

God does not want us to put death on his altar, but life. As his children, we are called to present our bodies as a *living sacrifice*. Choosing life is not only about *not* aborting when you get a positive pregnancy test. God wants us to *continue* to present our bodies as a sacrifice of life, for all of our days.

Far from having done our part when we carry a baby to term, we can continue to choose life every day. Every day we can choose the lives of others over our own lives. Every day we can lay down our desires, our selfish ambition, our self-importance, and choose life. And this sacrifice is not unique to mothers—all Christians can stand up for life by laying their own lives down.

Everyday Lives of Sacrifice

Right now, in our culture, in our time, there is something uniquely potent about mothers sacrificing for their children. As you lay down your life for your children, presenting yourself to God as a living sacrifice, that sacrifice makes an aroma. That aroma is a fragrance of life to God, but of contradiction to everything the world is fighting for. As you care for your children, as you discipline yourself, as you sacrifice yourself for them, even on the long days and tired moments, you are reaching out to the world. When you present yourself as a living sacrifice, the aroma of that sacrifice cannot be contained.

We do not turn toward our children and our homes because we do not care about the world. We turn inwards because the world needs to smell this sacrifice. It can be easy for mothers to feel like no one can see us in our daily labor, like our work doesn't really matter. We can feel like picketing outside of an abortion clinic is the only way to stop such horror, and we are unfortunately burdened with little children so we can't do it.

This is why I write for mothers about the small opportunities in the normal days. Not just because I think women need encouragement to love their children more. Not just because I think we need to value our own work and calling. But because the opportunities to choose life are with us all the time. It is a continuous choice. A choice that never naps and never stops growing; a choice that can only be made in faith, by the grace of a Savior who showed us how to live on an altar.

This Will Change the World

Motherhood is the big leagues of self-sacrifice. Millions of women kill to avoid it. In our culture of self-gratification, to embrace selfless motherhood is a revolutionary act. See the sacrifice, and rejoice in it. Recognize the cost is your life, and willingly lay yourself down. The world hates the smell of that sacrifice, because it is the smell of grace.

They hate it because it is the smell of something living and burning at the same time—something that is impossible without a risen Savior.

There is a time for standing on a sidewalk holding a sign, but holding a sign isn't what makes a mother pro-life. Being pro-life means putting the life of another ahead of your own. It means showing daily grace to the small souls nearest to you. It is not just an opinion or a position or a lobbyist group. It is the glory of maternal self-sacrifice that begins at conception and runs through labor and midnight feedings and diapers and sandwiches and crayons and homework and flu seasons and graduations and on into grandkids. It is an avalanche of small and large sacrifices. It burns bright in kitchens and bedrooms and backyards. Motherhood gives life to the pro-life movement, and it will change the world.

MOM ENOUGH

19 A Tantrum for My Transformation

CHRISTINA FOX

Some days I wake up and nothing seems to go right.

The alarm fails to sound. The kids are slow to get ready. The fridge is empty of milk (after I set the table with bowls of cereal). The route to an appointment is filled with red lights. The exam room is tiny and cramped, the wait is long, and the boys are full of energy. After the appointment, we stop at the grocery store on the way home (for the milk) and the boys act like wild animals escaped from a zoo. My heart sighs and I wish I could just rewind time and start the day all over.

What Should I Do?

Days like this would often leave me in despair. I felt frustrated, stressed, and overwhelmed. I desperately tried to figure out why my life was chaotic and how I could fix it. And then I felt guilty over my inability to do so. I thought that maybe I just needed to be more organized. If I could get control over the details of my life, maybe I wouldn't have such stressful days. I searched the blogs and read the books, hoping to find ways to make my life run smoothly, thinking the whole time that there must be something I can do—that there must be some way to grab back control over my days.

I need theology. I needed to know God deeply, and let his truth press deeply into my daily life. I realized that if I believe in the doctrine of God's sovereignty I had to face the truth that *God is never surprised by any frustrating event I encounter.* Spurgeon once said that even a speck of dust doesn't move unless God wants it to. God is in sovereign control of all he has made and of all the details of our lives. "Whatever the Lord pleases, he does, in heaven and on earth, in the seas and all deeps" (Ps. 135:6).

A Greater Plan for Me

Since this is true—since nothing happens outside God's will and plan—then all of my daily parenting challenges are under his sovereign control. He knows about the Target tantrums, the middle-of-the-night vomiting, and the bedtime battles. Sibling spats, markers on the walls, or potty training fiascos do not surprise him. All the events of our lives that feel out of our control are firmly within God's control.

Lamentations 3:37–38 says, "Who has spoken and it came to pass, unless the Lord has commanded it? Is it not from the mouth of the Most High that good and bad come?" Jerry Bridges comments on this passage, "God is in control of every circumstance and every event of our lives, and he uses them, often in some mysterious way, to change us more into the likeness of Christ."[7] What this means for me as a parent is that every late appointment and every empty jug of milk is sovereignly decreed and used for my good. *God uses my child's tantrum for my transformation.*

This truth has given me great freedom. Instead of despairing over the seemingly random and chaotic events in my life, I can view them in light of his sovereign care. When my days are long and everything seems to go wrong,

I know it has all happened for a reason. In fact, all of my parenting challenges are used for my spiritual good—they are to make me more like Christ (Rom. 8:28–29).

God is not in the business of making my life comfortable and free of stress. He has something greater planned for me: my holiness.

There Is Hope

In the midst of chaos, I see Jesus and how much I need the gospel every moment. The God of grace who saved me from sin is the God of grace who helps me show patience in the close confines of a pediatrician's office. Every challenging situation is an opportunity for me to trust him—to obey, to learn, to grow, to rely more on his grace.

So when the dryer breaks down and the van tire blows up, instead of despair we have hope. Life doesn't feel out of control if we know *Who* is in control. We can trust and rest in God's sovereignty, knowing that he uses our every stress for our transformation and his glory.

20 Kissing the Wave

GLORIA FURMAN

"How long, O Lord?" is a familiar cry to those who experience suffering and despair. In my own experience this question can be asked in both faith-filled hope and in faithless unbelief. I've asked it in both ways in the same hour.

Trials teach hard lessons, as Charles Spurgeon said: "I have learned to kiss the wave that throws me against the Rock of Ages."

Kissing the Wave?

What does Spurgeon mean, to learn to "kiss the wave"?

One thing he cannot mean is to call evil *good*. God's word forbids us to do such a thing: "Woe to those who call evil good and good evil" (Isa. 5:20). After he revealed his true identity to his brothers who had sold him into slavery, Joseph said, "As for you, you meant evil against me, but God meant it for good, to bring it about that many people should be kept alive, as they are today" (Gen. 50:20). Despite all of his hardship, Joseph was encouraged because he knew God was sovereign over his past, and he saw some of the good work God had already done through his trials.

Hindsight is 20/20, though, right? Where do we find comfort when we're in the thick of trials in which we can't see any good (at least not yet)? I think the answer to this question is also in Joseph's story.

Joseph's Story

There's a common thread that runs through each account of Joseph's ordeals, from being sold into Egypt as a slave to being wrongly incarcerated.

- "And the patriarchs, jealous of Joseph, sold him into Egypt; *but God was with him*" (Acts 7:9).
- "*The Lord was with Joseph*, and he became a successful man, and he was in the house of his Egyptian master" (Gen. 39:2).
- "His master saw that *the Lord was with him* and that the Lord caused all that he did to succeed in his hands" (Gen. 39:3).
- "But *the Lord was with Joseph* and showed him steadfast love and gave him favor in the sight of the keeper of the prison" (Gen. 39:21).
- "The keeper of the prison paid no attention to anything that was in Joseph's charge, because *the Lord was with him*. And whatever he did, the Lord made it succeed" (Gen. 39:23).

There's no doubt about it—the Lord was with Joseph. He was with Joseph in the pit. He was with Joseph in the house where he worked as a slave. He was with Joseph in jail. He was with Joseph in the court of Pharaoh. He was with Joseph in the most dramatic confrontation of his entire life. The waves kept throwing Joseph against the Rock of Ages.

God's Nearness

I don't think Spurgeon's comment came from a sarcastic "Pucker up waves!" perspective, but one of humble sobriety and childlike faith in God who works all things for our good. Whenever we encourage one another in our home with "kiss the wave," the words are often spoken into a tearful conversation as a lump rises in our throats.

The nearness of God is our good. And the trials we endure in this fallen world awaken us to this truth. We remember Jesus, who is called *Immanuel* ("God with us"), and the cross he bore for our sake. Can the waves of trials drown us if we have a Substitute who endured the greatest trial in our place?

We can "learn to kiss the wave" because Christ is near to us and because he is supremely sovereign over all things. He died and rose again to vanquish evil forever. Christ is our wisdom, righteousness, sanctification, and redemption (1 Cor. 1:30). You can't get much nearer than that.

When there's nothing in heaven or on earth or under the earth that can separate you from Christ's love, waves of trials can only throw you onto the Rock of Ages. Resting on that Rock is where I'd like to be and stay forever, and may the Lord bless the means he uses to remind me of that.

21 A Prayer for the Worried Mom's Heart

CHRISTINA FOX

Do you ever worry?

I think we can all admit that we do. In fact, we probably worry more than we realize. As a mother, I find myself worrying about my children, about their health, their learning, and whether I can just make it to bedtime each day.

I also find myself worried about our budget, about my husband's travel for work, and about the voicemail from my doctor. My to-do lists keep me awake at night because I fear I'll forget to do something important. Questions like "What if?" and "Should I?" swirl around my mind, holding me hostage and keeping me chained to my worries and fears.

Worry is a kind of "respectable sin." By that, I mean worry is one of those sins that everyone does, so we don't often address it. Like gossip, worry is something we all know we aren't supposed to do, but we often gloss over it and call it something else—something like *stress.* Especially for women, worry can even be expected.

But deep down, we want to be freed from the chronic feeling of doom and the expectation of something bad lurking just around the corner. We know that the Bible tells us not to worry, but "What if?" thoughts seem like such a part of us that we don't know how to stop.

What can we do?

Remember and Pray

Like oil and water, trust and worry do not mix. To expel worry from our heart, we must grow deep roots of trust in God. Time and again in the Psalms, when the writer's heart was heavy, he turned to look back at all that God had done for him. As the psalmist looked back at God's faithfulness and his sovereign care for him, he was able to trust God even in the midst of troubling circumstances.

When we look back at God's past faithfulness to us, it gives us confidence and hope in his future faithfulness. We look back to our own story of salvation. We see the demonstration of God's love for us when Jesus died on the cross for our sins. When worries threaten to seize our heart, we need to remember and dwell on the truth of the gospel. Remembering the cross propels us in faith for what lies ahead.

As we remember, we need to turn to God in prayer. Hebrews says that because of Jesus, we can come to the throne of grace with confidence, to receive the help we need (Heb. 4:16). Paul was referring to chronic worry when he wrote: "Do not be anxious about anything, but in everything by prayer and supplication with thanksgiving let your requests be made known to God" (Phil. 4:6). We can give our worries to God in prayer, trusting him with all our burdens and cares. As a result, we will receive in return the peace we long for, "And the peace of God, which surpasses all understanding, will guard your hearts and your minds in Christ Jesus" (Phil. 4:7).

We might even pray something like this. . .

A Prayer for the Worried Heart

My Papa in Heaven,
I come to you with a heavy heart full of so many

worries and cares. I want to just curl up on your lap and find some peace from the chaos in my life. My worries fill my mind night and day. My stomach is in knots and I can hardly breathe. I feel like I am drained dry; the joy has been sucked right out of me.

But you invite me to come with all these burdens. You said that you would carry them. You are my Rock, Shield, and Fortress. I need a Rock to stand on. I need a Shield to stand behind. I need a Fortress to run into. *I need you.*

There are so many decisions to make. What if I make the wrong one? So many bad things loom on the horizon. What if I'm not prepared? Help me to focus my heart on you and not on the giants around me. I know that all these worries are keeping me from trusting you. Like Peter, instead of looking toward your face, I am looking around at the waves encircling me.

Forgive me for doubting and not living a life of trust. I believe, but please help my unbelief! I know that when I worry, I believe a lie that says that I can control what happens in my life. Forgive me for trying to control something I never really had control of. Help me to trust in your word and not the lies.

You sent your Son to carry my greatest burden at the cross. I know that you can handle all that troubles me today. There is nothing too great for you. The earth is your footstool and the wind and rain come and go at your command. Free me of this worry today. Help me to trust the same grace that saved me at the cross to save me from all that weighs me down today.

I know that you have a perfect plan for my life. Help me to walk by faith and not by sight. I want to trust in your plan and your love for me. I want to face the unknown future, confident that you have it under control. Grant me the grace I need.

Thank you for Jesus and that because of him I can come to you in confidence. You accept me as I am, worries and all.

I give them all to you now,

In Jesus's name, Amen.

22 Our Children for Our Joy

TRILLIA NEWBELL

I dropped my son off at his school and yelled my usual goodbye through the open window: "I love you. Make good choices. Obey your teacher." As I began to roll up the window and drive away, my little first grader took his small hand to his mouth and blew me a kiss.

It was like everything stopped at that moment.

I realized how quickly this season will pass. Will he blow me a kiss when he's 16 years old? I don't know. I blew him a kiss back and he waved to me, mouthing the words "Bye, Mom." I was overwhelmed. I wished I could freeze that point in time.

Sweet Ragamuffins

I like to call my children "sweet ragamuffins." Motherhood is challenging, and my kids don't obey me every time I ask them to do something. They are rambunctious, loud, and messy. And they are sweet; they are treasures. Like many moms, I wouldn't trade motherhood for anything. What I think we can so often forget, though, is that motherhood isn't a task to be checked off like laundry. It is a calling.

Maybe the word "calling" makes you want to run and hide. For many, "calling" can sound as if motherhood is your only identity, an all-encompassing identity that is never relieved of an endless loop of responsibilities. This is not true. You are likely called to be a wife and church member and friend as well (and the list could go on). So motherhood is not your *only* identity, but it is an important part of your identity. And there is a weight to that. Mothers are more than just mothers, but we are never less. God's word instructs us to train up our children in the way they should go (Prov. 22:6). I can't think of a greater challenge. As one in the throes of raising and teaching young children, I am desperate for Jesus to help me in this challenging task.

Gifts to Enjoy

As we face the challenges of training our children, sometimes we focus more on the task than the treasure. Rather, remember, "every good gift and every perfect gift is from above, coming down from the Father of lights" (James 1:17). Our children are not tasks to complete, but gifts to enjoy. We enjoy them by remembering that they are truly gifts from God. Yes, even when they stand in the hall refusing to put away their socks, or when they throw their cereal on the floor, or when they hijack a trip to the grocery store. Yes, even in those moments, they are gifts.

Paul, instructing Timothy to challenge the rich to put their hope in God instead of wealth, reminds us that it is God who provides all things for our enjoyment (1 Tim. 6:17). Children are not to-dos to check off a list. They are to be delighted in. As with every gift we receive, we must be careful not to idolize our children. Only God should be worshipped. Instead, we must think of our kids as true gifts from God. As gifts, we enjoy something of God *in them*.

A Call to Treasure

I can think of many things I enjoy, but I value my kids

more. I love looking into the precious eyes of my kids. I want to get into the world of their God-given personalities and take in their laughs and answer their questions. I want to enjoy them.

Maybe that's precisely the main purpose of this mommy calling. Maybe it's not as much a call to *train* your kids as it is a call to *treasure* them.

Children change quickly. Let's enjoy these days that God has given us. They are his gifts, glimmers of his goodness, which leads us to say with C.S. Lewis, "What must be the quality of that Being whose far-off and momentary sparkles are like this!"

23 The Idols of a Mother's Heart

CHRISTINA FOX

When you are upset because you can't do something you want to do, it might be because that thing has become an idol in your heart.

I said these words one afternoon in response to one of my kids who was frustrated because I had taken away his highly valued time on the computer. We talked about how idols are not always easy to recognize, and that our emotional responses can sometimes indicate what is happening in our hearts.

Idols Specific to Motherhood

John Piper says God is most glorified in us when we are most satisfied in him. We were made to love and worship God. When God isn't the longing of our heart and the source of our satisfaction, we seek to fill our bellies somewhere else. Instead of filling the God-shaped hole in our hearts with enjoyment of him, we fill it with love for things, experiences, desires, and responses from others.

We often think of an idol as a manmade object that a person bows down and worships, but an idol can be anything that we love more than God. Idols consume our thinking and energy. Idols are so central to our lives that if we don't have them, we are devastated.

Motherhood has a unique set of idols. If you are a mother, you may recognize many or all of these.

Affirmation

This idol can include affirmation by friends and family, and even by strangers, that our children are "so well behaved" or "so talented." Pride can bubble up in our heart when we don't get the affirmation we want. Or when we receive correction and criticism, we get discouraged and frustrated. We also can seek affirmation through our children; their love for us can become an idol.

Children

Our children can become idols, too. Starting with even the desire to have children, which can become all consuming, even more important in our life than God. Once we have children, they can become idols when we live for them and always try to make them happy. We can seek to find our fulfillment in and through them. When they don't respond to us as we expect, or fail us in some way, we are devastated.

Success

We want our children to be successful because they reflect us. We may press them endlessly to excel. We may have in our minds an image of what a "perfect family" looks like, and until we have it, we feel like failures. Our children's limitations may shatter our dreams as well.

Control

Being in control of all the details of life is a big idol for many moms. We sanitize little hands, isolate them from runny noses, and strategize for unexpected events. We spend our days orchestrating every detail of our children's lives. But because nothing is actually in our control, we become anxious, worried, and agitated when things don't go as planned.

These are not the only idols a mother can have. In fact, the options for idolatry are endless. As John Calvin so memorably said, our hearts are idol-making factories. The question is not whether our hearts are manufacturing idols, but which ones.

Toppling Our Idols

I've worked with my children on identifying idols by having them cut out words and images of things that a person could love more than God, then gluing those images into a heart shape on a drawing of a person. We've done this activity a few times because it is helpful for them to see how much we fill our hearts with things other than God. One time, my son drew a frown on his person's face and said, "He is sad. All these things he loves haven't made him happy."

As moms, identifying our idols requires a little work. Like weeds, idols may have twisted themselves around our hearts, burrowing down deep into the recesses and crevices. They may have become such a part of our hearts that we have trouble recognizing them.

We have to pray that God will reveal the idols in our heart and help us to see and recognize them. Sometimes it helps to be aware of our emotional responses to the circumstances in our life. How do we react when our children let us down? How do we respond when we don't receive the affirmation from others that we desire? When God brings an idol to our attention, we have to humbly acknowledge our sin, repent, and turn away.

Turning *away* from our idols doesn't mean only turning away; we then have to turn *toward* something else. And that something else is the great Someone: Jesus. As Tim Keller writes,

> *Jesus must become more beautiful to your imagination, more attractive to your heart, than your idol. That is what will replace your counterfeit gods. If you uproot the idol and fail to "plant" the love of Christ in its place, the idol will grow back.*[8]

We can't simply try harder to avoid idols. We can't just resolve to resist them. We must focus our hearts on the person and work of Jesus. He must be the source of our satisfaction. We aim to desire him above all else. We want to dwell, meditate, and saturate our hearts with the truth of God's love and grace for us through the shed blood of Christ. The more we rest and trust in the gospel, the more our love for Christ grows until it overflows, drowning and washing away the idols in our heart.

24 Missional Motherhood

GLORIA FURMAN

The clarion call to repent and believe the gospel message reverberates all over the world. Evangelism is happening in remote jungles where missionary planes land on grass runways, in coffee shops set in the shadows of medieval architecture, in high-end boutiques in shopping malls, and in rickety taxis inching forward on congested roads.

We hear "missionary hero" stories and our hearts soar with thankfulness for the work the Spirit of God is doing all over the world. We pray for the "go-ers" and we cheerfully give our finances to send them.

But one brand-new mom told me with a sigh, "I want to 'go,' but I'm afraid the farthest I can 'go' these days is to the baby's crib and back." Many moms see their ministry to their children as insignificant when compared to other ministries. After all, crowds of thousands gather in open-air theaters and cheer to hear the gospel.

Because motherhood is missional, there's something of eternal value taking place in the realm of the unseen. It's true—sometimes the only cheering a mom hears is when the lid of the ice cream container snaps open in the kitchen. But as mothers faithfully raise up the next generation in the gospel, the applause of heaven echoes in eternity.

Missions and Motherhood

We can find four specific encouragements for missional motherhood in 2 Corinthians 4.

First, we get a grip on being a jar of clay. No mother can claim to have it all together. Being a fragile, common jar of clay means that we are free to enjoy and appropriate the sufficient grace of God and show the world that "the surpassing power belongs to God and not to us" (see 2 Cor. 4:7–10). Because Christ's strength is made perfect through our weakness, we are free to lose the pretense that we are self-sufficient moms. Instead, we can boast all the more gladly of our weaknesses so that the power of Christ may rest on us and fuel our contentment (2 Cor. 12:9–10).

Second, we learn to stamp eternity on our eyeballs. It sounds like a fancy contact lens, but this phrase comes from a prayer attributed to Jonathan Edwards. Missional motherhood takes the long view, stretching way past the last diaper purchase (though we might pray that the Lord would hasten *that* day). The perspective we need looks past all the earthly milestones in our children's lives and into eternity. The eyes of our heart are fixed on forever, "knowing that he who raised the Lord Jesus will raise us also with Jesus and bring us with you into his presence" (2 Cor. 4:14).

Eternity reminds us that our children are not "mere mortals," as C.S. Lewis described in his essay "The Weight of Glory." But every human being is God's image bearer with an eternal soul. Motherhood is missional because no mom has ever taught a mere mortal about how "hands are for helping and not hitting," or wiped sweet potatoes off a mere mortal's face, or prayed for a mere mortal before school, or listened to a mere mortal tell a drawn-out story about the pigeon on the balcony.

Eternity means that childrearing is an awe-full, serious *joy*.

Third, we get goose bumps thinking about how God's grace is extending to more and more people. Missional motherhood knows all too well that we are nurturing life in the face of death. Grace, gratitude, and glory are not light and trite ideas in this world filled with the stench of death and blighted by the marks of reprehensible sin. The aim of *all* our work is that grace will extend to more and more people, increase thanksgiving to God, and glorify him (2 Cor. 4:15).

Our work as moms is to glorify God, who sent his Son to do *his* mighty work on the cross in our place to pay the just penalty for our sins. Humbly receiving God's grace and inviting our children to share our joyful gratitude for what Jesus has done on the cross is our happy mission in this fallen world.

Fourth, we joke about getting younger on our birthdays, but we laugh because we've got something better. Even as our "outer self" experiences the inevitable entropy of age, Jesus is renewing our "inner self" day by day (2 Cor. 4:16). The best place to find this renewing strength is in God's word. Over all the helpful, how-to mom advice, we receive wisdom from above in the Bible. Moms know they need to be near to God and understand just how near he is to them.

So through his word, "God daily comes to his people, not from afar but nearby. In it he reveals himself, from day to day. . . . Scripture is the ongoing rapport between heaven and earth, between Christ and his church, between God and his children. It does not just tie us to the past; it binds us to the living Lord in the heavens. It is the living voice of God."[9]

Soundtrack of Heaven

Missional motherhood is no stranger to the challenges of nurturing life in the face of death, while dying to self every day. But missional motherhood sees with eyes of faith a glimpse of something soul-steadying and bright—a "weight of glory" (2 Cor. 4:17). That weight of glory is far heavier than the twelve-kilo toddler who keeps climbing on top of the counter and getting stuck.

All over the world, it is only by the grace of God that moms can nurture the souls of our littlest neighbors. All the while the soundtrack of heaven is ringing in our hearts: "Salvation belongs to our God who sits on the throne, and to the Lamb!   . . . Amen! Blessing and glory and wisdom and thanksgiving and honor and power and might be to our God forever and ever! Amen" (Rev. 7:10, 12).

Endnotes

1   Michael Oh, conference message, "Missions as Fasting" (February 4, 2009).
http://www.desiringgod.org/conference-messages/missions-as-fasting

2   Nancy Wilson, *The Fruit of Her Hands: Respect and the Christian Woman*
(Canon: 1997), 58.

3   I base my parable on the parable of Jesus in Luke 18:9–14.

4   Glenna Matthews, *"Just a Housewife": The Rise and Fall of Domesticity in
America* (Oxford: 1989), 6–7.

5   Margaret Sanger, *Woman and the New Race* (1920), 232–234.

6   Jonathan Parnell, blog post, "Embracing Weakness Will Change Your Life"
(February 28, 2013). http://www.desiringgod.org/blog/posts/embracing-
weakness-will-change-your-life

7   Jerry Bridges, *Respectable Sins: Confronting the Sins We Tolerate* (NavPress:
2007), 44.

8   Timothy Keller, *Counterfeit Gods: The Empty Promises of Money, Sex, and
Power, and the Only Hope that Matters* (Dutton: 2009), 172.

9   Herman Bavinck, *Reformed Dogmatics* (Baker: 2008), 1:385.

✳ desiringGod

Everyone wants to be happy. Our website was born and built for happiness. We want people everywhere to under-stand and embrace the truth that *God is most glorified in us when we are most satisfied in him*. We've collected more than thirty years of John Piper's speaking and writing, including translations into more than forty languages. We also provide a daily stream of new written, audio, and video resources to help you find truth, purpose, and satisfaction that never end. And it's all available free of charge, thanks to the generosity of people who've been blessed by the ministry.

If you want more resources for true happiness, or if you want to learn more about our work at Desiring God, we invite you to visit us at www.desiringGod.org.

desiringgod.org

17490304R00069

Made in the USA
San Bernardino, CA
11 December 2014